Jay

New Action Sports

Snowboarding Basics

by Jackson Jay

CAPSTONE PRESS

MANKATO

C A P S T O N E   P R E S S

818 Willow Street • Mankato, MN 56001

Printed in the United States of America.

Library of Congress Cataloging-in-Publication Data
Jay, Jackson
    Snowboarding basics / Jackson Jay.
      p. cm.
    Includes bibliographical references and index.
    Summary: Introduces the history, equipment, techniques, and competitions
    of the relatively new sport of snowboarding.
    ISBN 1-56065-401-5
    1. Snowboarding--Juvenile literature. [1. Snowboarding.] I. Title
GV857.S57J39   1996
796.9--dc20   95-44718
                                                                CIP
                                                                AC

Photo credits

F-Stock: p. 17; Mark Gallup: pp. 4, 13, 15, 25, 33, 34; Larry Pierce: p. 7;
    Kevin Syms: p. 16; Kirk Anderson: p. 26; A. Anderson: pp. 28-29; Eric
    Sanford: pp. 30, 36; David Wheelock: pp. 40-41.
Cheryl Richter: pp. 8, 21, 22, 42.
Visuals Unlimited: Mark E. Gibson: pp. 10, 18; W. Banaszewski, p. 39.

Table of Contents

Words in **boldface** type in the text are defined in the Glossary in the back of the book.

Chapter 1

Shredders

Surfers and skateboarders never liked winter. When the weather turned cold and snow began to fall, they had to give up their sports. They had to wait for warm weather to return.

But surfers and skateboarders do not have to wait anymore. Now, when winter comes, they pull out a snowboard and start **shreddin'**.

Shreddin' is what snowboarders call their sport. It is one of the fastest growing sports in the world.

Snowboarding started at downhill ski areas.

Wide, Short Board

Snowboarders call themselves **shredheads**. They use a board that looks like a wide, short water ski. They strap their boots to the board. Then they take off down a hill.

Snowboarding started at ski areas. Skiers and some resort owners did not welcome the shredders at first. The shredders were different. They were fast. People worried about crashes and injuries. They thought the shredders were wild and crazy kids.

Over time, though, a lot of skiers tried snowboarding. Many of them loved it. People also learned that the number of snowboarding injuries is about the same as for skiing. So the bad feelings have died down.

Seeing a snowboarder is common now. Snowboarding is still done mostly at ski areas.

There are almost 2 million snowboarders on the slopes today.

Skiers used to think snowboarders were just wild and crazy kids.

There are almost 2 million snowboarders on the slopes today. There were only a few thousand in the early 1980s.

History

The first snowboard was called a Snurfer. It was invented in the mid-1960s. It was like a water ski with a short rope attached to the front. The rider held the rope and stood on it like a skateboard or surfboard.

It was like trying to ride a toboggan standing up. It was hard to stay on. It was almost impossible to turn.

Over the years, people made homemade snowboards. Many of them were skateboarders. Tom Sims was one of them. He built a snowboard in 1963 as a project for his shop class. Today, Tom is the owner of Sims Snowboards in Vancouver, British Columbia.

Another early snowboarder was Jake Burton. He offered boards and lessons as early as 1977. His company, Burton Snowboards, is now one of the largest. A lot of the ideas to improve snowboards and snowboarding equipment came from Burton.

Chapter 2

Equipment

Y ou do not need much equipment to snowboard. You need a board, boots, bindings, and warm clothes.

Board

Renting a snowboard is a good idea for your first few trips. You can try out different types and sizes of boards. Eventually you will find one that is right for you.

The best snowboards are made of wood strips glued together. These are called laminates.

A lot of boards are made of wood strips glued together. These are called wood **laminates**. Most shredders think wood laminate makes the best boards.

Snowboards are getting lighter and longer-lasting. New glues keep the boards more stable than the older glues did. The new boards do not wear out as fast.

Snowboards are measured in centimeters. They vary in length from 110 centimeters to 180 centimeters. Boards also come in different widths. It is important to choose the length and width best for you. You do not want your toes or heels to hang over the edge. You also do not want a board that is too wide. It will be hard to steer.

You need to pick a board with the right **flex**. Flex is how the board bends. A soft board is good for doing tricks. But it is not as stable. A stiff board is good for beginners. It is easier to control.

Snowboarders wear comfortable clothes that will keep them warm and dry.

Boots

There are special boots made just for snowboarding. But regular winter boots will work with some bindings, as long as the boots are snug.

Snowboarding boots are not like hard, stiff ski boots. They are flexible but also give some

13

ankle support. Your boots should be snug. Snug boots let you feel and control the board. But they should not be too tight. Tight boots make your feet uncomfortable and cold.

The newest types of boots are called linerless boots. They are lightweight. They have less ankle support and no liner for warmth. They are great for **freestyle** snowboarding.

But linerless boots are not for **freeriding**. They are not for the beginner. Beginning snowboarders need more foot and ankle support.

Bindings

Bindings keep your boots attached to the snowboard. Most bindings have two or three

Snowboarding is one of the fastest growing sports in the world.

straps. They have a stiff, high back to support your lower leg.

Beginning boarders may change their **stance** as they get to be better shredders. They might want to get adjustable bindings. Bindings do not come with the boards. They have to be purchased separately.

Step-ins are the newest kind of bindings. With step-ins, shredders do not have to sit in the snow to fit and fasten their straps. They just slide their feet right in.

Most injuries happen in the first two days of snowboarding.

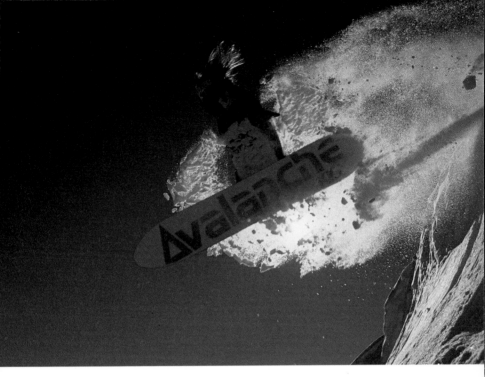

It is easy to lose control of a snowboard.

Clothing

Snowboarders should wear comfortable clothes that are warm and dry. Clothes should be loose enough to move around in.

Stylish snowboarders wear bright, baggy outfits. Special pants with extra padding in the seat cushion them when they fall.

Chapter 3

How to Snowboard Safely

The fastest way to learn the basics of snowboarding is to take a lesson. Many ski resorts offer lessons from professional shredders.

Most lessons start with getting used to the board. There are two ways to stand on a board. They are regular foot and goofy foot.

Your stance is regular when you stand with your left foot in front and your right foot in

Your stance can be either regular foot or goofy foot.

back. Your stance is goofy foot when you stand with your right foot in front and your left foot in back. Neither way is better than the other way. What matters it that your stance feels comfortable.

Once you are on a board, you will know which stance you like. If you are a skateboarder or surfer, you already know. Skateboarders, surfers, and snowboarders use the same stances.

Learning to Fall and Stop

Snowboarders fall a lot. You need to learn to fall properly. Most injuries happen in the first two days of snowboarding. Most are wrist or thumb injuries. Most injuries come from trying to break a fall.

The best way to fall is to hold your elbows in. Let your forearms take the shock. Do not

Most ski areas offer snowboarding lessons.

20

hold your arms out. Do not land on your hands. You could break your wrists.

It is easy to lose control of a snowboard. Until you get the hang of it, do not be shy about falling on purpose. Falling on purpose is called bailing out. It may prevent injuries.

To stop when you are losing control, simply sit down.

Snowboarders have to strap on some kinds of bindings. They can just step into other kinds.

Getting Started

Here is how to get started. Strap your front foot into the binding. Push yourself forward with your back foot and glide. Ride the snowboard like you would ride a skateboard. Do not put your back foot on the board yet.

Your back foot will help you keep your balance. You can drag it to stop. It is important to learn to ride the board with just your front foot. You will ride with one foot when you get on and off a ski lift.

Control

You control the snowboard by shifting your weight toward your toes or toward your heels. You will move in the direction that you shift your weight.

Skateboarders and surfers shift their weight in the same way. But on a snowboard your feet are in bindings. You cannot move them around like a surfer or skateboarder can.

Turns

The key to riding a snowboard is learning frontside and backside turns. Your toes are on the frontside of the board. Your heels are on the backside.

Shift your weight to your toes to do a frontside turn. Push down with your heels to do a backside turn. Find your balance and learn to use just the right amount of pressure.

Do one turn and then the other as you head down the slope. You will carve the letter S in the snow.

Hit the Bunny Slopes

Start snowboarding on easy slopes. They are called bunny slopes. The bottom 40 feet (12 meters) of a bunny slope is a good place to practice.

Practice your S curves. Get the feel of the flex of your board. Try bending your knees.

Even the best snowboarders started on the bunny slopes.

This adds pressure to the board. When you add pressure, you **weigh** the board. **Unweigh** the board by straightening up.

Try weighing and unweighing the board while you make S curves. Notice the difference. Weighing and unweighing will help you make good, quick turns. Weighing and unweighing will help you when you learn tricks.

Most beginner lessons end on the bunny slope. Give yourself plenty of time to learn the basics.

You will probably find yourself on the ground a lot. Do not worry about it. Everybody falls, especially at the beginning. Brush yourself off and get back to it.

Weighing and unweighing the board will help you learn tricks.

You do not need snow to snowboard. Some people practice on sand. (Photo next page)

Chapter 4

Snowboard Competitions

The first big snowboarding contest was held during the 1981-82 ski season in Colorado. Since then, many more competitions have been held.

In 1995, Stratton Mountain in Vermont held its 12th annual U.S. Open Snowboarding Championship. There is a good chance that

Snowboard teams are sponsored by equipment makers.

snowboarding will be a medal sport at future Olympic games.

Two major snowboarding organizations sponsor national competitions every year. One is the United States Amateur Snowboard Association (USASA). The other is the United States Snowboard Association (USSA).

Snowboarders come to the competitions from many different countries. Some belong to teams. The teams are sponsored by equipment makers.

There are four events in most snowboard competitions. Two are speed events and two are freestyle events. The speed events are downhill racing and slalom. The freestyle events are **half-pipe** and slope-style.

Some racers reach speeds of 70 miles (112 kilometers) per hour.

Downhill

The downhill is the fastest race. Boarders go down the mountain as fast as possible. They have to maintain control through the turns. Some racers reach 70 miles (112 kilometers) per hour.

The boards used for the downhill are stiffer than those used for slalom. The stiffness makes the boards more stable at high speeds.

Slalom

In a slalom race, boarders weave between poles. Very quick turns are necessary. Racers need speed and control to make the best times.

In a dual slalom, two boarders race. There are two sets of poles. They are put up side-by-side. The boarders weave between the poles. Boarders are out of the race if they fall or miss a pole.

Racers need speed and control to make the best times.

Boards for the slalom have more flex than boards for the downhill. They are often much shorter, too.

Half-pipe

The half-pipe comes from the world of skateboarding. The half-pipe is a wide chute in the snow with curved sides. It looks like giant pipe cut in half.

Half-pipe events are contests of tricks and style. Half-pipe shredders build up speed and fly into the air. They do tricks on their way down.

One trick is called an ollie. It is a jump into the air. Riding backwards is called a fakie. A tailgrab is when you grab the back of the board while you are in the air.

Judges give points for the boarders' performances. Sometimes points are lost if

Almost all ski resorts allow snowboarding.

boarders go too slow, fall, or are not smooth enough.

Boards for the half-pipe are often the lightest boards. They have the most flex.

Slope-style

Slope-style is another judged event. It takes place in a snowboard park. Boarders score points for the tricks they do. They are also judged on how good they look as they perform.

Some slope-style boarders do the moguls. Moguls are large bumps on the slope. They are made of packed snow. Slopes with moguls are fun and challenging.

Some boarders weave through them like a speeding snake. Others pop off the moguls and fly into the air like ski jumpers. Racers try to get through the moguls as fast as possible without falling or crashing.

The Future

Snowboarding is now a worldwide sport. More and more skiers are trying out snowboards.

A snowboarder takes a jump over some friends.

Almost all ski resorts allow snowboarding. Many ski areas even feature snow parks with special runs just for boarders.

If you want to be good enough to compete, it will take practice. If you do not want to compete, that is fine, too.

Most snowboarders shred for fun. For shredders, the first snow is a welcome visitor. One they hope will stay a long time.

Glossary

flex—the ability of a board to bend

freeriding—riding all over a mountain, not just in a park or on one trail

freestyle—trick snowboarding

half-pipe—a chute dug in the snow with curved sides like half a pipe

laminates—thick wood made by gluing together thin layers of wood

shreddin'—snowboarding, especially with speed and style

shredheads—people who snowboard

stance—the way you stand on a snowboard

unweigh—to take pressure off the snowboard

weigh—to press down on the snowboard

A snowboard looks like a wide, short water ski.

To Learn More

Althen, K.C. *The Complete Book of Snowboarding.* Rutland, Vt.: Charles E. Tuttle, 1990.

Brimner, Larry Dane. *Snowboarding.* New York: Franklin Watts, 1990.

Dieterich, Michele. *Skiing.* Minneapolis: Lerner Publications, 1992.

Lurie, Jon. *Fundamental Snowboarding.* Minneapolis: Lerner Publications, 1996.

McMullen, J. *Basic Essentials of Snowboarding.* Merrilville, Ind.: ICS Books, 1991.

Videos

Snowboarding. Costa Mesa, Calif.: Unreel
Productions, 1987.

Snow Shredders. Costa Mesa, Calif.: Unreel
Productions, 1988.

You can read articles about snowboarding in
the following magazines: *Snowboarding*,
Snowboarder, and *Snowboard Life*.

Useful Addresses

Canadian Ski Association (CSA)
1600 James Naismith Drive
Gloucester, ON K1B 5N4
Canada

North American Snowboard Association
P.O. Box 38836
Denver, CO 80238

**United States Amateur Snowboard
  Association**
P.O. Box 251
Green Valley Lake, CA 92341

U.S. Snowboarding
c/o U.S. Skiing
Box 100
Park City, UT 84060

Index